BUGS

What is a bug?

The word "bug" is commonly used to describe many different types of creepy-crawlies. Spiders, bees and centipedes are all bugs! We can divide bugs into groups depending on their body and the number of legs they have.

Arachnids

Spiders, scorpions, ticks and mites are all arachnids. They have eight legs, no antennae and their body is made up of two parts: a cephalothorax (head and thorax combined) and an abdomen.

Banded Demoiselle Dragonfly

Myriapods

Millipedes and centipedes are myriapods. They have more than eight legs – in fact, some have more than 300 legs! Their body is made up of two parts: a head and a trunk.

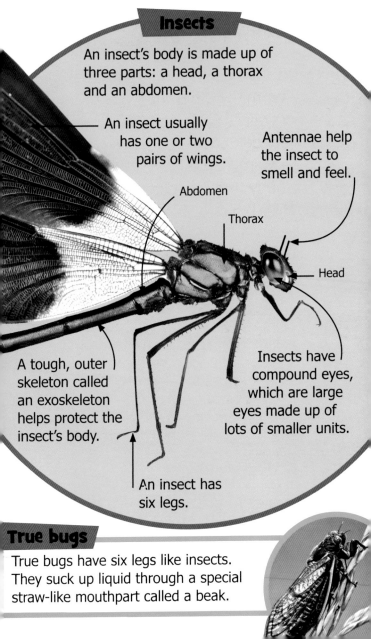

Insects

An insect's body is made up of three parts: a head, a thorax and an abdomen.

An insect usually has one or two pairs of wings.

Antennae help the insect to smell and feel.

Abdomen

Thorax

Head

A tough, outer skeleton called an exoskeleton helps protect the insect's body.

Insects have compound eyes, which are large eyes made up of lots of smaller units.

An insect has six legs.

True bugs

True bugs have six legs like insects. They suck up liquid through a special straw-like mouthpart called a beak.

True bugs

All true bugs are insects, but unlike most insects, they have a tube-like mouthpart called a beak to pierce and suck up liquid food. Most true bugs also have wings, although some are wingless.

Stink bugs

Shield bugs are also called stink bugs because they produce a bad smell when they feel threatened.

A true bug uses its beak like a straw to stab and suck up food.

Other true bugs

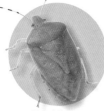

Shield Bug

Cicada

Bed Bug

6

The shield bug gets its name because its body is shaped like a shield.

Assassin bugs

An assassin bug lies in wait before attacking its prey and injecting it with a poisonous saliva. This stops the prey from moving and breaks down its insides until they are soft. The assassin bug sucks up the prey's insides, leaving just the skin behind.

A colourful pattern warns predators not to attack.

Lantern Bug

Aphid

Beetles

There are many different types of beetle. They make up almost a quarter of all the animal species on Earth. Beetles usually have two pairs of wings, and like all insects, they have a hard exoskeleton.

When the ladybird isn't flying, the tough front pair of wings fold over the softer hind wings, protecting them.

Mandibles

Mandibles

Ladybirds feed on bugs like aphids using jaws called mandibles.

Other beetles

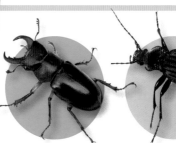

Rhinoceros Beetle

Stag Beetle

Ground Beetle

8

The ladybird's brightly coloured body warns other animals that it is poisonous and will not taste very nice!

Ladybird

A ladybird's hind wings are so thin that you can see through them.

Beetles use their legs to move around, swim, jump and even dig.

Antennae help the ladybird to smell, taste and feel.

A helping hand

Many beetles can help humans. Ladybirds eat aphids – pests that damage plants. Dung beetles use animal droppings, which they roll into a ball using their strong legs.

Tiger Beetle

Ants

All over the world, ants live together in large groups called colonies. Many species of ant live in rainforests. A colony of ants is like a very organised family, where every ant has its own job to do.

Thorax

Head

Antennae help ants to hear, touch, taste and smell. Ants can give out different smells to warn each other of danger ahead.

Some ants bite using strong jaws called mandibles.

Nests

Ants build nests in mounds, underground and in trees. A nest contains tunnels and chambers that have been dug out by the workers.

Abdomen

An ant colony may have one or several queen ants to lay eggs. The queen mates with male ants – this is the male ants' only job. There can be hundreds of thousands of worker ants in a colony and they are always female. They have many jobs, including working on the nest, protecting the colony, looking for food and caring for the eggs.

Red Ant

Other ants

Army Ants

Black Garden Ant

Leaf-Cutter Ant

Caterpillars

Butterflies and moths begin life as caterpillars. They hatch from the eggs laid on leaves by the adults. Caterpillars eat constantly, getting bigger and bigger, until they are ready to pupate, which means to turn into an adult butterfly or moth.

The caterpillar has strong jaws for eating.

The front pairs of legs are called thoracic legs. They are for walking and gripping hold of things.

A Monarch caterpillar grows up

A butterfly lays eggs under a leaf.

A caterpillar hatches from the egg, eats and eats, and grows.

The caterpillar makes a silk pad to grip on to.

New skin

A caterpillar's skin does not stretch much. When it is too small, the skin breaks, and the caterpillar crawls out. Underneath, there is a new, larger skin.

A caterpillar's body is divided into 13 segments.

Swallowtail Butterfly Caterpillar

Caterpillars have different numbers of prolegs depending on the family they are from.

The caterpillar uses its prolegs to cling to plants.

The caterpillar's skin splits to reveal the chrysalis.

Inside the chrysalis, the caterpillar changes.

An adult butterfly breaks out of the chrysalis.

13

Butterflies

Beautiful butterflies can often be seen basking in the warmth of the sun. If they get too cold, they cannot move to find food or escape from attackers.

Antennae allow the butterfly to smell as well as sense the direction it is travelling in.

Compound eyes can see in red, yellow and green.

Butterflies drink using a long, straw-like tube called a proboscis.

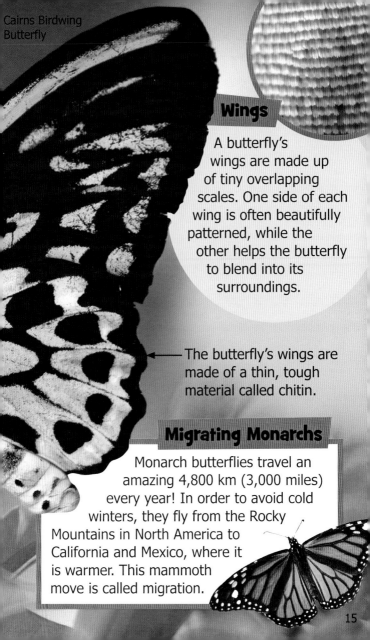

Cairns Birdwing
Butterfly

Wings

A butterfly's wings are made up of tiny overlapping scales. One side of each wing is often beautifully patterned, while the other helps the butterfly to blend into its surroundings.

The butterfly's wings are made of a thin, tough material called chitin.

Migrating Monarchs

Monarch butterflies travel an amazing 4,800 km (3,000 miles) every year! In order to avoid cold winters, they fly from the Rocky Mountains in North America to California and Mexico, where it is warmer. This mammoth move is called migration.

Flies

House flies, mosquitoes, midges and gnats are all types of true flies. Flies can be so tiny that they are barely visible or as long as 5 cm (2 in). They are fantastic fliers and can hover, fly backwards and fly upside down!

Most flies have one pair of wings, although some are wingless.

Large, compound eyes help the fly to see in all directions.

When a fly rubs its feet together, it is getting rid of dirt to keep its feet clean!

House Fly

Harmful flies

Mosquitoes bite humans and spread malaria, which is a deadly disease. Other flies carry the germs of diseases and leave them on our food.

A fly's wings can show bright colours that appear to change in different light.

Hover Fly

Haltere

Halteres

Halteres are like tiny drumsticks behind the fly's wings. They help the fly to balance when it flies.

Helpful flies

Some flies spread pollen from flower to flower, like bees do, while other flies help us to remove waste. They do this by laying their eggs on rotting food or dead animals. This provides their grubs with food to eat.

Bees

There are thousands of different types of bee. Most of them live alone, but some, like the honey bee, live in big groups in a nest, or hive. They fill the hive with honey, which provides food for all the bees.

Bees have excellent eyesight.

Honey Bee

Pollen from the flowers sticks to the honey bee's body. The bee combs it into pollen baskets on its back legs. Pollen provides food for the young bees.

Queens and workers

Every hive has a queen bee who lays the eggs. Most of the bees are worker bees, who look after the eggs and gather nectar from flowers. The workers use straw-like mouthparts to suck up the nectar, which they then use to make honey.

Queen Bee

Bees have two pairs of wings.

Life in a hive

Young worker bees make wax, which they use to construct the honeycomb.

The queen bee lays each egg in a cell of the comb. When the eggs hatch, the worker bees feed the larvae.

Only female bees have a sting. It is found in their tail.

The larvae grow and grow and then change into adult bees.

Dragonflies

The colourful dragonfly may look beautiful, but it is a fearsome hunter. The dragonfly uses all of its legs and its jaws to hold on to its prey. It can even eat while it is flying.

Life cycle of a dragonfly

A dragonfly nymph hatches from an egg under water, or near water. It can swim, but it can't fly because it doesn't have wings yet.

The nymph grows and sheds its skin many times.

The new adult dragonfly crawls out of the water and waits for its wings to dry and harden.

The dragonfly flies away to feed and find a mate.

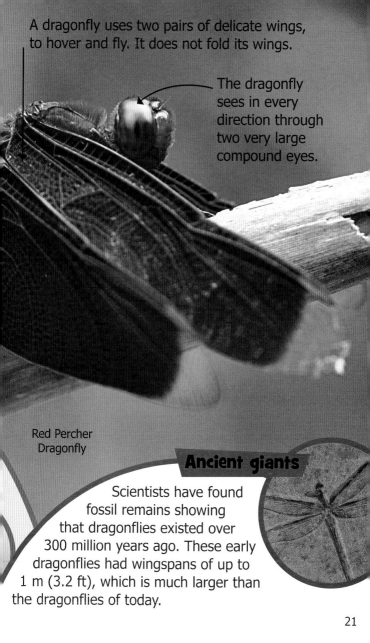

A dragonfly uses two pairs of delicate wings, to hover and fly. It does not fold its wings.

The dragonfly sees in every direction through two very large compound eyes.

Red Percher Dragonfly

Ancient giants

Scientists have found fossil remains showing that dragonflies existed over 300 million years ago. These early dragonflies had wingspans of up to 1 m (3.2 ft), which is much larger than the dragonflies of today.

21

Mantids

The mantid is an excellent hunter and will eat many insects, including other mantids. It is also called a "praying mantis" because its folded legs make it look as though it is praying.

If a mantid feels threatened, it will fan out its wings to appear bigger.

Spiky legs

A mantid uses two large compound eyes to estimate how far away its prey is before striking.

A mantid uses spikes on its front legs to hold its prey before chewing it up alive.

A mantid can turn its triangular head almost all the way around to look for prey.

Common Green Praying Mantis

Praying mantids are experts in disguise. A green or brown body makes it easy for them to blend in or camouflage with their surroundings so that they can hide in wait for their prey.

Blending in

Spiders

All spiders are arachnids. They can spin strong silk from spinnerets at the back of their abdomen and can even coat their silk to make it waterproof.

Sensitive hairs on the spider's body help it to feel the world around it.

Silk spinners

Spiders use their silk to create webs, to make traps and nests, to wrap up their prey and to secure themselves as they jump from place to place. Some spiders can even spin underwater webs to hold an air bubble so that they can breathe.

Feeler →

Mexican Red Kneed Tarantula

Other spiders

Black Widow Spider

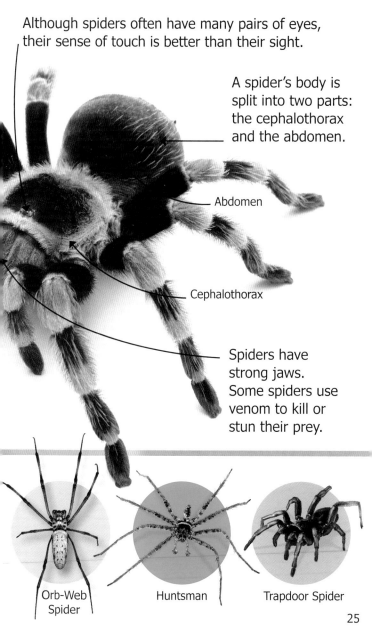

Although spiders often have many pairs of eyes, their sense of touch is better than their sight.

A spider's body is split into two parts: the cephalothorax and the abdomen.

Abdomen

Cephalothorax

Spiders have strong jaws. Some spiders use venom to kill or stun their prey.

Orb-Web Spider

Huntsman

Trapdoor Spider

25

Scorpions

Scorpions use powerful pincers and a sting to catch their prey. A few species can kill humans using the venom in their sting. The scorpion is an ancient creature that has lived on Earth for hundreds of millions of years!

Eyes

Cephalothorax

Scorpions are arachnids. They have eight legs.

Powerful pincers grab and hold on to the prey.

Give me a ride!

Female scorpions give birth to live babies. Unlike other bugs, the female scorpion takes care of her babies by carrying them on her back until they are strong enough to look after themselves.

The scorpion raises the sting over its head to stab its prey. It injects a venom, which can kill some animals instantly.

Emperor Scorpion

Abdomen

A scorpion's body is split into two parts: the cephalothorax and the abdomen.

Survival experts

Many scorpions live in areas like the desert, where food is hard to find. To survive, the scorpion can slow down everything in its body and manage to live on just one insect a year!

Scorpions don't have very good eyesight, so they use sensitive hairs on their body to help sense the world around them.

Centipedes and millipedes

Both centipedes and millipedes have bodies made up of segments and many pairs of legs. Centipede means "hundred feet" and millipede means "thousand feet". Neither bug necessarily has that number of legs, but they can have as many as 750!

Common Centipede

Long antenna

Each segment has one pair of legs attached to it.

The common centipede has a flat body. It can grow to about 30 mm (1.1 in) long.

Centipedes are meat-eaters. They use their first pair of legs like claws to stab their prey and inject venom.

Eating habits

Centipedes eat other bugs and can even eat small animals like mice! A few millipedes are meat-eaters, but most feed on dead or dying plants – making them helpful recyclers!

A redbanded millipede has a rounded body. It can grow to about 150 mm (6 in) long.

Short antenna

Each segment has two pairs of legs attached to it.

Redbanded Millipede

Coil up

Millipedes can coil into a spiral to protect themselves from attack. This means that their soft underside is kept safe. Millipedes also give off a smelly substance to drive off predators.

29

Glossary

This glossary explains some of the harder words in the book.

abdomen The back part of a bug's body.

antennae The pair of feelers on a bug's head, used to smell, taste and sense movement.

camouflage When something hides by blending into its surroundings.

cephalothorax A head and thorax that are joined together to make one body part. Spiders have a cephalothorax.

chitin The tough, protective material that makes up an insect's exoskeleton.

chrysalis The pupa of a butterfly. It is not held within a cocoon.

cocoon A silk case that moths and some other insects spin around the pupa.

colony A group of one kind of animal or plant that lives and works together.

exoskeleton A tough outer covering or shell that helps to protect an insect's body.

grub An insect larva. Sometimes a grub looks like a maggot or a caterpillar.

honeycomb The wax structure made up of lots of holes, in which bees store honey and eggs.

larva A young insect before it has changed into its adult form. A caterpillar is the larva of a butterfly.

nectar A sugary liquid made by flowers.

nymph A young dragonfly or other insect that changes into its adult body without being held in a case or cocoon.

pincer The front claw of animals like scorpions, crabs and lobsters.

predator An animal that hunts and eats other animals.

prey An animal that is hunted and eaten by another animal.

proleg A leg attached to the abdomen of insects like caterpillars.

pupa The stage in an insect larva's life when it is changing from a larva to an adult insect.

pupate The act of changing from an insect larva to an adult insect.

spinneret The part of a spider or other bug that makes silk thread.

thorax The middle part of an insect's body to which the legs and wings are joined.

venom A poisonous liquid made by scorpions and other animals.